Daily Spar

MW01289451

The New And Proven Concept To Speak Spanish In 45 Days

By

Octavio Méndez

Table of Contents

Introduction

Have you ever asked yourself why should you learn Spanish? Spanish is one of the three most spoken languages in the world. Even if you live in a place where everyone speaks English, you will need Spanish sometimes. If you plan to travel to a Spanish-speaking country, you will need to learn the basics to enjoy your trip to the fullest.

One of the biggest problems when learning a new language is the time it takes and sometimes, we do not have it since life is full of things to do. On the other hand, many beginners wonder where to start. Maybe you have several options to choose from, but when something is about investing time and money, you will consider it very well, right?

For this reason, thinking about your valuable time, I have decided to create this *Daily Spanish Lessons Book* which is designed to learn a little Spanish everyday in just a few minutes! Are you looking for a simple and effective way to learn Spanish? If your answer is *yes*, this book is definitely your best choice.

Some of its characteristics are simplicity, easy to understand, useful, and reliable. This book contains a vocabulary section that will help you to learn new Spanish words and phrases everyday, as well as a grammar explanation that will allow you to understand and learn the grammatical structure and enjoy speaking good Spanish from the beginning.

After having studied this guide, you will be able to communicate and make yourself understood in different fields of daily life. In addition, you will be trained to deepen the learning.

This book aims to introduce you to the beautiful world of this language and I am sure it will be your starting point to explore and learn the basic terms to communicate with Spanish-speaking people and avoid common mistakes that some English-speaking people make when learning Spanish. Even if you have never had contact with Spanish before, this book is perfect for you because it is for people with very little or no knowledge of Spanish.

Do not shrink from starting as soon as possible, this book is structured by a day-to-day learning, so you´ll only need ten minutes daily, and after you have read this manual you will feel more secure and eager to practice what you have learned.

Do not wait any longer, start now and you´ll see that thanks to this guide, it has never been so pleasant and easy to learn a new language and improve your grammar skill.

Greetings

Day 1. Vocabulary And Phrases

Here are some common words and phrases that are used frequently when you meet people for the first time or subsequent.

Saludos Greetings

¡Hola! Hello!

¡Buenos días! Good morning!

¡Buenas tardes! Good afternoon!

¡Buenas noches! Good night! / Good evening!

¿Cómo estás? How are you?

Estoy bien, gracias. I´m fine, thanks.

Más o menos. More or less.

¡Adiós! Goodbye!

¡Hasta luego! See you later!

¡Hasta mañana! See you tomorrow!

¡Por favor! Please!

¡Muchas gracias! Thank you so much!

¡De nada! You´re welcome!

¡Bienvenido! Welcome!

¡Lo siento! I´m sorry!

¡Disculpa! Excuse me!

Por favor, habla despacio. Please, speak slowly.

¿Cómo te llamas? What is your name?

Mi nombre es My name is

Mucho gusto. Nice to meet you!

Mucho gusto en conocerte también. Nice to meet you too.

Este es mi amigo. This is my friend (male friend).

Esta es mi amiga. This is my friend (female friend).

¿De dónde eres? Where are you from?

Yo soy de Puerto Rico. I am from Puerto Rico.

Nací en Nueva Zelanda. I was born in New Zeland.

¿Dónde vives? Where do you live?

Yo vivo en I live in

Saludos a María. Say Hello to María.

Atentamente. Best regards.

Eres muy amable. You´re very kind.

Te veo la próxima semana. See you next weekend.

¡Cuídate! Take care!

Te presento a mi jefe. I introduce you to my boss.

Ella es de Colombia. She is from Colombia.

Él es muy amable. He is very kind.

Me cae muy bien. I really like him.

Tu español es muy bueno. Your Spanish is very good.

¡Felicidades! Congratulations!

¡Buena suerte! Good luck!

¡Lo haces muy bien! You do it very well.

Day 2. Verb To Be *(Ser / Estar)*

The verb **ser** is used to describe characteristics of an

object or a person, to talk about time and dates.

The verb **estar** is used to talk about location, to describe the physical state of a person or thing, and to describe feelings.

Below are the different conjugations of the verb **ser** & **estar** in the present tense (Am, Are, Is).

Yo soy / estoy I am

Tú eres / estás You are

Él / Ella es / está He / She is

Nosotros somos / estamos We are

Ustedes son / están You are

Ellos / Ellas son / están They are

Questions: ¿*Ser / Estar* + Subject + C?

¿*Está tu hijo enfermo?* Is your son sick?

¿*Son tus zapatos negros?* Are your shoes black?

¿Está Lucía en casa? Is Lucía at home?

¿Es tu papá el nuevo gerente? Is your dad the new manager?

Affirmative sentences: Subject + *Ser / Estar* + C.

Mi hijo está enfermo. My son is sick.

Mis zapatos son negros. My shoes are black.

Lucía está en casa. Lucía is at home.

Mi papá es el nuevo gerente. My dad is the new manager.

Negative sentences: Subject + *no* + *Ser / Estar* + C.

Mi hijo no está enfermo. My son is not sick.

Mis zapatos no son negros. My shoes are not black.

Lucía no está en casa. Lucía is not at home.

Mi papá no es el nuevo gerente. My dad is not the new manager.

Day 3. Past Tense Of Verb *Ser*

Verb Ser in Past tense (Was/Were)

The verb **Ser** has a different meaning in Spanish and the past form is **Yo fui** or **Yo era.** It´s simpler than you think, you just have to learn some easy rules.

Imperfect Tense Form: describe a past moment, express continuity and what is happening at that moment, actions that were done frequently and regularly.

Yo era I was

Tú eras You were

Él / Ella era He / She was

Nosotros éramos We were

Ustedes eran You were

Ellos eran They were

Example:

1. ***Mi abuelo era italiano***. My grandfather was Italian. (Past moment, but it doesn´t stop being)

2. ***Mi madre era una mujer hermosa.*** My mother was a beautiful woman. (past moment)

3. ***Nosotros éramos los mejores jugadores***. We were the best players. (Action done frequently)

4. ***Eran los mejores alumnos de su escuela.*** They were the best students in their school. (past moment)

5. ***Tú eras el chico más popular.*** You were the most popular boy.

6. ***Cuando eras una niña jugabas con muñecas.*** When you were a girl you played with dolls.

Preterite Indefinite Form: express a past and finished action, to list past actions.

Yo fui I was

Tú fuiste You were

Él / Ella fue He / She was

Nosotros fuimos We were

Ustedes fueron You were

Ellos fueron They were

Example:

1. ***Mi abuela fue médica***. My grandmother was a medic/doctor. (past and finished action)
2. ***Yo fui vendedor cuando era joven.*** I was a salesman when I was young.
3. ***Mateo fue un buen hombre.*** Mateo was a good man.
4. ***Mi padre fue un excelente esposo.*** My father was a great husband.
5. ***Yo fui la ganadora del premio.*** I was the winner of the prize.
6. ***Fuimos socios y amigos cuando trabajamos juntos.*** We were partners and friends when we worked together.

Day 4. When To Use *Ser*

Professions:

Mi mamá fue una buena arquitecta. My mom was a good architect.

Yo soy abogada. I am a lawyer.

Ellos son buenos médicos. They are good doctors.

Michael es un buen pintor. Michael is a good painter.

Descriptions:

Su casa es hermosa. Her house is beautiful.

Mi hermano es alto y flaco. My brother is tall and thin.

Cuando era joven me gustaba correr. When I was young, I liked to run.

El jardín es grande y bonito. The garden is big and nice.

Possession:

Las maletas son mías. The suitcases are mine.

Esta es mi casa, bienvenido. This is my house, welcome!

Ella es mi prima. She is my cousin.

Él es mi perro Toby. He is my dog Toby.

Nationality:

Yo soy mexicano. I am Mexican.

Ellos son europeos. They are European.

Ella es africana. She is African.

Nosotros somos americanos. We are Americans.

To Ask for Price:

¿Cuánto es? How much is it?

¿Es este el precio? Is this the price?

¿Crees que es muy caro? Do you think it is very expensive?

¿Es barato? Is it cheap?

To Give the Price:

Son 20 dólares. It is 20 dollars.

Ese era el precio. That was the price.

Es barato. It is cheap.

Era muy caro. It was very expensive.

Date:

Ayer fue nuestro aniversario. Yesterday was our anniversary.

Las reuniones son los martes. The meetings are on Tuesdays.

Hoy es mi cumpleaños. Today is my birthday.

El mes pasado fue nuestra boda. Our wedding was the last month.

Time:

Son las 5:00 en punto. It´s 5 O´clock.

La cita es a las 3:30 pm. The appointment is at

3:30 pm.

Nos vemos a las 6:15 pm. See you at 6:15 pm.

El accidente fue anoche a las 10. The accident was at 10 last night.

<u>More examples where you must use the verb ***Ser***</u>:

1. ***La puerta principal de mi casa es negra.*** The main door of my house is black.
2. ***La chica es alta y rubia.*** The girl is tall and blond.
3. ***Hoy es lunes, tengo examen de historia.*** Today is Monday, I have a history exam.
4. ***Los cachorros son encantadores.*** The puppies are lovely.
5. ***Los estudiantes son muy inteligentes.*** Students are very smart.
6. ***Él es un buen cirujano***. He is a good surgeon.
7. ***Ellos son millonarios, son los dueños de esta empresa***. They are millionaires, they are the owners of this company.

8. ***El lugar donde vivo es muy agradable***. The place where I live is very nice.

9. ***Los tomates son muy baratos en este mercado.*** Tomatoes are very cheap in this market.

10. ***Mi familia es pequeña.*** My family is small.

Day 5. When To Use *Estar*

Location:

El libro está sobre la mesa blanca. The book is on the white table.

El hospital está al norte de la ciudad. The hospital is in north of the city.

Las maletas están en el carro. The suitcases are in the car.

Estoy en el aeropuerto de Miami. I am at the Miami Airport.

Feelings:

Los vecinos están preocupados por el

accidente. The neighbors are worried because of the accident.

Estamos felices de verte. We are happy to see you.

Mis abuelos están enojados contigo. My grandparents are angry with you.

Los niños están muy cansados. The children are very tired.

More examples where you must use the verb *Estar:*

1. *El aeropuerto está en Madrid.* The airport is in Madrid.
2. *El carro de mi esposo está sucio.* My husband´s car is dirty.
3. *El Banco Nacional está cerrado*. The National Bank is closed.
4. *Mi esposo está feliz porque lo promovieron.* My husband is happy because he was promoted.
5. **Estoy embarazada y estamos muy felices**. I am pregnant and we are very happy.

6. **La carretera está bloqueada por el accidente.** The highway is blocked because of the accident.

7. **Mi casa está cerca del supermercado**. My house is close to the supermarket.

8. **La caja de madera está en el armario.** The wooden box is in the closet.

9. **Estamos en el parque con los niños**. We are in the park with the children.

10. **Ellos están muy enamorados.** They are so in love.

Day 6. Personal Pronouns

Personal pronouns indicate the grammatical person and they usually refer to people, animals, or objects.

Yo I

Tú You

Él He

Ella She

Nosotros-as We

Ustedes You

Ellos / Ellas They

There are three of the singular form and three of the plural form:

Singular Person: **Yo, Tú, Él / Ella**

1. **Yo soy una buena maestra.** I am a good teacher.
2. **Tú eres mi mejor amigo**. You are my best friend.
3. **Él es nuevo en la clase**. He is new to the class.
4. **Ella es mi cuñada**. She is my sister-in-law.

Plural Person: **Nosotros, Ustedes, Ellos / Ellas.**

1. **Nosotros somos Ingleses.** We are English.
2. **Ustedes son buenos vecinos.** You are good neighbors.
3. **Ellos son los mejores jugadores.** They are the best players.

4. **Ellas son las dueñas de la propiedad**. They are the owners of the property.

Important: In Spanish, unlike English, we can generally omit the pronoun, but there are some exceptions: when you want to emphasize the subject and when by the context, the subject is not explicit.

More Examples:

1. **Te presento a Juan. [Él] es mi hermano mayor.** I introduce you to Juan. He is my older brother. (You have made it clear that you mean Juan.)

2. **Laura y yo trabajamos juntas, [nosotras] somos buenas amigas.** Laura and I work together, we are good friends. (You have made it clear that you mean both, you and Laura.)

3. **Ellos son mis profesores.** They are my teachers. (If you want to emphasize the subject.)

4. ***[Tú] eres un buen ejemplo de valor.*** You are a good example of courage. (You are talking to someone else directly, so the subject is obvious.)

5. ***[Yo] tengo muchas pecas en mi cara.*** I have many freckles on my face. (The conjugation of the verb **"tengo"** lets you know who is being talked about.)

6. ***[Nosotros] llegamos primero que ustedes.*** We arrived first than you. (The conjugation of the verb **"llegamos"** lets you know who is being talked about.)

7. ***Nosotros llegamos primero.*** We arrived first. (If you want to emphasize the subject, that <u>we</u> arrived first than the others.)

8. ***Ellos son muy fuertes.*** They are very strong. (To emphasize the subject or if it is not explicit.)

9. ***¿Irán [ustedes] al baile esta noche?*** Will you go to the dance tonight? (You are talking to someone else directly, so the subject is obvious.)

10. ***[Nosotros] vamos a pasar recogiendo a Mario, [él] está enfermo.*** We are going to pick Mario up, he is sick.

Day 7. Possessive Pronouns

They are used to talk about the thing possessed and *must match the noun.* There are possessive adjectives that are placed before the noun or after the noun.

<u>*Before* the Noun, Singular/Plural</u>

<u>Yo.</u> *Mi / Mis* My

<u>Tú.</u> *Tu / Tus* Your

<u>Él / Ella.</u> *Su / Sus* His / Her

<u>Nosotros.</u> *Nuestro-a / Nuestros-as* Our

<u>Ustedes.</u> *Su / Sus* Your

<u>Ellos.</u> *Su / Sus* Their

<u>Example:</u>

1. ***Ella es mi cuñada, somos buenas amigas.***
   She is my sister-in-law; we are good friends.

2. ***Ellos son mis hijos, son gemelos.*** They are my children, they are twins.

3. ***Soy amiga de tus padres.*** I am a friend of your parents.

4. ***Me gusta ver a los niños con sus uniformes.*** I like to see children with their uniforms.

5. ***Mi computadora está apagada.*** My computer is turned off.

6. ***Tu carro es grande y cómodo.*** Your car is big and comfortable.

7. ***El papá de su novio tuvo un accidente.*** Her boyfriend´s father had an accident.

8. ***Él trajo sus cosas para trabajar.*** He brought his things to work.

9. ***Nuestras botas están húmedas.*** Our boots are wet.

10. ***Nuestro trabajo está a tres horas de nuestra casa.*** Our work is three hours from our house.

After the noun, singular/plural

Yo *Mío-s* / *Mía-s* Mine

Tú *Tuyo-s / Tuya-s* Yours

Él / Ella *Suyo-s / Suya-s* His / Her

Nosotros *Nuestro-a / Nuestros-as* Ours

Ustedes *Suyos / Suyas* Yours

Ellos *Suyos / Suyas* Theirs

Example:

1. *El sombrero negro es mío.* The black hat is mine.
2. *Las camisas que están en mi bolso son mías.* The shirts that are in my bag are mine.
3. *Ella envió la invitación a cada persona, esta es tuya.* She sent the invitation to each person, this is yours.
4. *Estos libros son suyos.* These books are yours.
5. *Ese celular es tuyo.* That cellphone is yours.
6. *Las lámparas son tuyas.* The lamps are yours.
7. *La maleta que está dentro del carro es suya.* The suitcase inside the car is hers.
8. *Nos llevaremos las nuestras a casa.* We will take ours to our house.

9. ***Este pantalón es <u>tuyo</u>.*** These pants are yours.

10. ***¡Son las <u>nuestras</u>!*** They are ours!

More Examples:

1. ***Nuestros perros son unos cachorros.*** Our dogs are puppies.

2. ***Este es mi cinturón.*** This is my belt.

3. ***Nuestros amigos están de vacaciones.*** Our friends are on vacation.

4. ***Nuestras hijas viven en Canadá.*** Our daughters live in Canada.

5. ***Son sus perros***. These are their dogs.

6. ***Él es su esposo***. He is her husband.

7. ***Es un regalo de sus nietos***. It is a gift from their grandchildren.

8. ***Fue un gusto conocer a tu esposa***. It was nice to meet your wife.

9. ***Me gustan mis zapatos, pero los tuyos están bonitos también.*** I like my shoes, but yours are beautiful too.

10. ***Lleva tu abrigo porque hará mucho frío.*** Take your coat because it will be very cold.

Numbers

Day 8. Vocabulary

Número Number

Número de teléfono Phone number

Número de celular Cellphone number

Matemáticas Maths

Fecha Date

Cumpleaños Birthday

Vacaciones Holidays

Sumar To add

Contar To count

Restar Substract

Multiplicar Multiply

Dividir Divide

Mes Month

Rico Rich

Semana Week

Calcular To calculate

Es demasiado. It´s too much.

¿Cuántos hay? How many are there?

Es muy poco. It´s very little.

Calculadora Calculator

Day 9. Cardinal Numbers

Cardinal numbers are used to count things They refer to quantity and correspond to the name of the exact number that we want to say.

0 *Cero* Zero

1 *Uno* One

2 *Dos* Two

3 *Tres* Three

4 *Cuatro* Four

5 *Cinco* Five

6 *Seis* Six

7 *Siete* Seven

8 *Ocho* Eight

9 *Nueve* Nine

10 *Diez* Ten

11 *Once* Eleven

12 *Doce* Twelve

13 *Trece* Thirteen

14 *Catorce* Fourteen

15 *Quince* Fifteen

16 *Dieciséis* Sixteen

17 *Diecisiete* Seventeen

18 *Dieciocho* Eighteen

19 *Diecinueve* Nineteen

20 *Veinte* Twenty

21 *Veintiuno* Twenty-one

22 *Veintidós* Twenty-two

23 *Veintitrés* Twenty-three

24 *Veinticuatro* Twenty-four

25 *Veinticinco* Twenty-five

30 *Treinta* Thirty

40 *Cuarenta* Forty

50 *Cincuenta* Fifty

60 *Sesenta* Sixty

70 *Setenta* Seventy

80 *Ochenta* Eighty

90 *Noventa* Ninety

100 *Cien* One Hundred

200 *Doscientos* Two Hundred

300 *Trescientos* Three Hundred

400 *Cuatrocientos* Four Hundred

500 *Quinientos* Five Hundred

1,000 *Mil* One Thousand

1,000,000 *Un millón* One Million

Example:

1. ***¿Cuál es tu número de teléfono?*** What is your cellphone number?

2. ***Mi número de teléfono es uno ocho tres cuatro nueve cero cinco seis.*** My phone number is 1834-9056.

3. ***Hay tres manzanas en la nevera.*** There are three apples in the fridge.

4. ***Trabajo ocho horas todos los días.*** I work eight hours everyday.

5. ***Mi jefe me dio cien dólares por mi trabajo.*** My boss gave me one hundred dollars for my work.

6. ***No me gustan las matemáticas.*** I do not like mathematics.

7. ***Hay quinientas personas en el salón, son demasiados.*** There are five hundred people in the room, they are too many.

8. ***Por favor calcula el número de invitados.*** Please calculate the number of guests.

9. ***El noventa por ciento de la población habla inglés y español.*** Ninety percent of the population speaks English and Spanish.

10. ***Habrá descuentos del 50% el fin de semana.***

There will be 50% discounts this weekend.

Day 10. Ordinal Numbers

Ordinal numbers are used to describe an order in situations, people or objects.

1ro ***Primero*** First

2do ***Segundo*** Second

3ro ***Tercero*** Third

4to ***Cuarto*** Fourth

5to ***Quinto*** Fifth

6to ***Sexto*** Sixth

7mo ***Séptimo*** Seventh

8vo ***Octavo*** Eighth

9no ***Noveno*** Nineth

10mo ***Décimo*** Tenth

11mo ***Undécimo*** Eleventh

12mo **Duodécimo** Twelfth

13ro **Décimotercero** Thirteenth

14to **Décimocuarto** Fourteenth

20mo **Vigésimo** Twentieth

21ro **Vigésimoprimero** Twenty First

30mo **Trigésimo** Thirtieth

100mo **Centésimo.**Hundredth

Important: In Spanish, **Primero** and **Tercero** change when they go before a masculine noun.

Example:

1. **Ayer publiqué mi tercer libro.** I published my third book yesterday.
2. **Es el tercero en la fila.** He is the third in the line.
3. **Vendí mi primer carro muy barato.** I sold my first car very cheap.
4. **Esa fue mi primera casa, la compré con mi primer salario.** That was my first house, I bought it with my first salary.

5. ***Ganó el <u>segundo</u> lugar en la competición de fútbol.*** He won the second place in the soccer competition.

6. ***Ella es su <u>segunda</u> hija, se llama Julia.*** She is her second child; her name is Julia.

7. ***Estamos celebrando nuestro <u>vigésimo</u> aniversario de matrimonio.*** We are celebrating our twentieth anniversary of marriage.

8. ***Hoy es su <u>cuarta</u> noche en el hospital.*** Today is his fourth night in the hospital.

9. ***El fue mi <u>primer</u> maestro en la escuela.*** He was my first teacher at school.

10. ***Vamos a celebrar nuestro <u>tercer</u> año juntos en la compañía.*** We will celebrate our third year together in the company.

Day 11. Prepositions I

Prepositions serve as a link between two elements of the sentence. The most common in Spanish are:

A To /At /By

De Of /From

Desde Since

Con With

Por By

En In /On

Entre Between

Para For

Sobre On /About

Durante During

Después de After

Antes de Before

How to Use Prepositions

A: For the hours of the day, to describe a position or location (to a place), to describe a way by which something is done.

Example:

1. ***Haré ejercicios a las 8:00 am***. I will do exercises at 8:00 am.

2. ***Voy a viajar a Brasil***. I´m going to travel to Brazil.

3. ***La chica va a casa***. The girl goes home.

4. ***Ellos irán a pie***. They will go by foot.

5. ***Hecho a mano***. Made by hand/handmade.

6. ***Abrimos el negocio todos los días a las 7 de la mañana***. We open the business everyday at 7 o´clock in the morning.

7. ***Saldremos a comer esta tarde***. We will go out eating this afternoon.

8. ***Los niños van a la escuela todas las tardes.*** Children go to school every afternoon.

9. ***Iremos a Panamá el próximo mes***. We will go to Panama next month.

10. ***Llegaré tarde a casa***. I will be late at home.

De: To indicate the start of something, the origin of something or someone, to indicate that something belongs to someone, what material something is made.

Example:

1. *Mi clase es de 7 a 9*. My class is from 7 to 9.

2. *Yo soy de Australia*. I am from Australia.

3. *Él es amigo de mi Hermana*. He is a friend of my sister.

4. *Este carro es de mi papá*. This car is from my dad.

5. *Mi cartera es de cuero*. My wallet is made of leather.

6. *Las camisetas son de algodón*. T-shirts are made of cotton.

7. *Es un libro de Darío*. It is a book of Darío.

8. *Soy el administrador de la tienda.* I am the store manager.

9. *Somos de México, un país grande*. We are from Mexico, a big country.

10. *Ellos son los abuelos de mi novio.* They are my boyfriend´s grandparents.

*Important: **A** and **De** can be contracted when are*

followed by a definite article.

Example:

a + el = al

1. **Voy al [a el] baño**. I go to the bathroom.
2. **Vamos al [a el] hospital.** We go to the hospital.

de + el = del

1. **Es la moto del [de el] vecino**. It's the neighbor's motorbike.
2. **Saldré del [de el] país el día quince del próximo mes.** I will leave the country on the fifteenth day of the next month.

Day 12. Prepositions II

Desde: When something begins at a certain time.

Example:

1. ***Desde que lo conocí, es mi mejor amigo.*** Since I met him, he is my best friend.

2. ***Trabajo en el Banco Central desde 1999.*** I work in the Central Bank since 1999.

3. ***Estoy en el hospital desde el domingo.*** I am in the hospital since Sunday.

4. ***El mercado está abierto desde las 6 de la mañana.*** The market is open from 6 in the morning.

5. ***Sus problemas empezaron desde que llegó ella.*** Their problems started since she arrived.

6. ***Estoy con este tratamiento desde el año pasado.*** I am with this treatment since last year.

7. ***Teníamos que hablar desde el principio.*** We had to talk from the beginning.

8. ***Somos amigos desde que estudiamos en la Universidad.*** We are friends since we studied at the University.

9. ***Estoy aquí desde las 2 de la tarde y aún no me atienden.*** I am here since 2 o´clock in the afternoon and they still do not take care of me.

10. ***Estoy viviendo en Nueva York <u>desde</u> el año pasado.*** I am living in New York since last year.

Con: When you want to explain that someone is in the company of another person or thing.

Example:

1. ***Estoy <u>con</u> mi perro***. I am with my dog.
2. ***Iré al cine <u>con</u> mis amigos***. I will go to the cinema with my friends.
3. ***Se casará <u>con</u> Juan.*** She will marry John.
4. ***¿Te gusta comer arroz <u>con</u> camarones?*** Do you like to eat rice with shrimps?
5. ***Quiero ir al mar <u>con</u> mi familia.*** I want to go to the sea with my family.
6. ***Tengo que viajar a Londres <u>con</u> mi jefe.*** I have to travel to London with my boss.
7. ***Necesito hablar <u>con</u> ustedes sobre algo importante.*** I need to talk to you about an important issue.

8. *La torta con helado es deliciosa.* The cake with ice cream is delicious.

9. *Siempre hago ejercicios con mi música favorita.* I always do exercises with my favorite music.

10. *Estaré con mi papá este fin de semana.* I will be with my dad this weekend.

Por: For moments of the day, places that one passes through, the way you make something, to explain the reason or cause of something.

Example:

1. *Los niños estudian por la mañana.* Children study in the morning.

2. *Te veré por la noche.* I will see you at night.

3. *Tendrás que pasar por los Estados Unidos.* You´ll have to go through the United States.

4. *Envió la carta por correo electrónico.* She sent the letter by e-mail.

5. ***No pude salir por la lluvia***. I couldn´t leave because of the rain.

6. ***Pasaré por la librería antes de ir a tu casa***. I will go through the bookstore before going to your house.

7. ***Lo hago por mi familia***. I do it for my family.

8. **Iré a visitar a Pablo por la noche.** I will go to visit Pablo at night.

9. ***El sábado por la mañana estaré en una reunión.*** I will be in a meeting Saturday morning.

10. **Llegaré tarde por la tormenta.** I will be late because of the storm.

Day 13. Prepositions III

En: To say that something is inside or directly on something.

Example:

1. ***Las frutas están en el carro.*** The fruits are in the car.

2. *Estoy en mi casa.* I am at home.

3. *El libro está en la silla*. The book is on the chair.

4. *Los niños están en su habitación*. The children are in their room.

5. *Mi esposa no está en casa.* My wife is not at home.

6. *El teléfono está en la mesa.* The telephone is on the table.

7. *El enfermo está en el hospital.* The patient is in the hospital.

8. *Tengo una casa en la ciudad.* I have a house in the city.

9. *Ellos están en el mismo salón*. They are in the same living room.

10. *Las compras están en el carro.* The shopping is in the car.

Entre: When something is between two or more things.

Example:

1. *México está entre Estados Unidos y Guatemala.* Mexico is between the United States. and Guatemala.

2. *La víctima está entre la vida y la muerte.* The victim is between life and death.

3. *La cocina está entre la sala y el comedor*. The kitchen is between the living room and the dining room.

4. *Coloca el queso entre ambos panes*. Place the cheese between both breads.

5. *Panamá está entre Costa Rica y Colombia*. Panama is between Costa Rica and Colombia.

6. *El avión está volando entre las nubes*. The plane is flying through the clouds.

7. *El cantante está entre la multitud.* The singer is among the crowd.

8. *Estamos entre amigos, puedes hablar con confianza.* We are among friends; you can speak with confidence.

9. *Coloca la mesa entre el pasillo y la habitación.* Put the table between the hall and the bedroom.

10. ***Mira la foto, tú estas <u>entre</u> mi hermano y yo.*** Look at the picture, you are between my brother and me.

Para: To refer to the recipient, to say the reason why you use something.

Example:

1. ***Compré un regalo <u>para</u> mi novia***. I bought a present for my girlfriend.
2. ***Estos zapatos son <u>para</u> tí.*** These shoes are for you.
3. ***Necesito una cama <u>para</u> dormir.*** I need a bed to sleep.
4. ***Esa silla es <u>para</u> descansar.*** That chair is for resting.
5. ***Voy a dormir bien <u>para</u> levantarme con más energía.*** I will sleep well to wake up with more energy.
6. ***Compré comida <u>para</u> toda la semana***. I bought food for the whole week.

7. **Mi traje está listo para mañana**. My suit is ready for tomorrow.

8. **Compré medicina para mi abuela**. I bought medicine for my grandmother.

9. **Envié un paquete para Carlos.** I sent a package for Carlos.

10. **Hice mi tarea para mañana.** I did my homework for tomorrow.

Day 14. Prepositions IV

Sobre: On top of something, to talk about something or the highest position.

Example:

1. **El bolso está sobre la cama.** The bag is on the bed.

2. **El discurso era sobre la pobreza.** The speech was about poverty.

3. **Sobre la cima de las montañas**. Over the top of the mountains.

4. *La investigación es sobre medicina natural.* The research is about natural medicine.

5. *Mi tarea es sobre los animales salvajes.* My homework is about wild animals.

6. *El ave está sobre la rama.* The bird is on the branch.

7. *Esas casas están sobre las montañas.* Those houses are on the mountains.

8. *El gato está sobre tu cama.* The cat is on your bed.

9. *Coloca el papel sobre la mesa.* Put the paper on the table.

10. *La biografía es sobre su infancia.* The biography is about his childhood.

Durante: For a period of time.

Example:

1. *Voy a estar fuera durante una semana.* I will be out for a week.

2. **Estuve en Canadá durante todo el curso**. I was in Canada during the whole course.

3. **Estuvimos de visita durante un mes.** We were visiting for a month.

4. **Estuve viviendo en Madrid durante mucho tiempo.** I was living in Madrid for a long time.

5. **Estaremos de vacaciones durante dos semanas.** We will be on vacation for two weeks.

6. **Mi doctor me envió reposo durante tres meses.** My doctor sent me to rest for three months.

7. **Mis primos están en un curso durante dos días.** My cousins are in a course for two days.

8. **Estuvimos en el congreso durante ocho horas.** We were in the congress for eight hours.

9. **La niña estuvo sin comida durante 24 horas.** The girl was without food for 24 hours.

10. **Estarán en su casa de campo durante el fin de semana.** They will be in their country house during the weekend.

Después de: After a specific moment in time.

Example:

1. ***Iré al gimnasio después del trabajo.*** I will go to the gym after work.

2. ***Comeremos después de las 9.*** We will eat after 9.

3. ***Iré después de tí***. I´ll go after you.

4. ***El postre es después de la comida.*** The dessert is after the meal.

5. ***Primero haz la tarea y después podrás jugar***. First, do the homework and then you could play.

6. ***Tomaré una siesta después del almuerzo.*** I will take a nap after lunch.

7. ***Visitaré a mis padres después de hacer las compras.*** I will visit my parents after doing shopping.

8. ***Iremos a celebrar después de tu ascenso***. We will go celebrate after your promotion.

9. ***Vamos a llevar a los niños al cine después de la escuela.*** We will take the children to the movies after school.

10. ***Estás _después de_ mí en la lista***. You are after me on the list.

Antes de: Previously at a certain time.

Example:

1. ***Cepilla tus dientes _antes de_ dormir***. Brush your teeth before going to sleep.
2. ***Me lavo las manos _antes de_ comer.*** I wash my hands before eating.
3. ***La ciudad era muy bonita _antes del_ terremoto***. The city was very beautiful before the earthquake.
4. ***Hoy desperté _antes de_ que mi alarma sonara.*** Today I woke up before my alarm rang.
5. ***Limpiaré mi casa _antes de_ salir***. I will clean my house before leaving.
6. ***Te dare un té de hierbas _antes de_ dormir.*** I will give you an herbal tea before sleep.
7. ***Ordena tu habitación _antes de_ salir.*** Tidy your room before leaving.

8. ***Deberías tomar la pastilla <u>antes de</u> desayunar***. You should take the pill before having breakfast.

9. ***Estaremos ahí <u>antes de</u> las 6 pm***. We will be there before 6 pm.

10. ***No deberías hacer ejercicios <u>antes de</u> dormir***. You should not do exercises before sleeping.

Address

Day 15. Vocabulary

Calle Street

Carretera Highway / Road

Ciudad City

Pueblo Town

País Country

Camino Path

Barrio / Vecindario Neighborhood

Rotonda Roundabout

Parque central Central park

Calle principal Main street

Banco Central Central bank

Hospital Hospital

Villa Small town

Playa Beach

Mercado Market

Cuadra Block

Metros Meters

Kilómetros Kilometers

Millas Miles

Cerca Near

Lejos Far / Far away

En frente de In front of

Contigüo a / Al lado de Next to

Esquina opuesta Opposite corner

Acera / Vereda Sidewalk

Ve despacio Go slow

Parada de bus Bus stop

Estación Station

Mapa Map

Brújula Compass

Example:

1. *La farmacia está en frente del parque central.* The pharmacy is in front of the central park.

2. *La tienda está contigüa al banco*. The grocery shop is next to the bank.

3. *La ferretería está en la esquina opuesta del supermercado.* The hardware store is on the opposite corner of the supermarket.

4. *La calle principal está muy concurrida.* The main street is very busy.

5. *La carretera está bloqueada.* The road is blocked.

6. *Mi casa está a doscientos metros de la playa*. My house is two hundred meters from the beach.

7. *Mis abuelos viven cerca de mi casa*. My grandparents live near my house.

8. *El hospital está lejos de tu trabajo.* The hospital is far from your work.

9. *La velocidad máxima es 80 kilómetros por hora.* The máximum speed is 80 kilometers per hour.

10. ***Estoy cerca de la rotonda***. I am near the roundabout.

Day 16. Cardinal Points & Addresses

Norte North

Sur South

Este East

Oeste West

Noreste Northeast

Noroeste Northwest

Sureste Southeast

Suroeste Southwest

Dos cuadras al Norte Two blocks north.

Cien metros al Sur One hundred meters south

Segunda calle Noroeste 2nd street northwest

¿Cuál es tu dirección? What is your address?

Mi dirección es _. My address is _.

Yo vivo en _. I live in _.

Camina directo a Walk straight to

Gira a la derecha Turn right

Gira a la izquierda Turn left

Regresar / Girar Turn around

Camina 100 metros hacia adelante Walk 100 meters forward

Retrocede 200 metros Go back 200 meters

Day 17. Conjunctions Y/E/O/U

Y

Conjunctions are links between sentences or words. The conjunction *"y"* means addition and is regularly used when you add or list something. When the word that follows the conjunction begins with *i / hi*, we´ll use *"e"*.

Example:

1. ***Compré fresas, uvas y naranjas. Fui al banco e hice algunos pagos.*** I bought

strawberries, grapes, and oranges. I went to the bank and made some payments.

2. *Juan e Isabel salieron a cenar*. John and Isabel went out to dinner.

3. *María y Luis están de vacaciones en Fiyi*. Maria and Luis are on vacation in Fiji.

4. *Ayer y hoy he estado en casa*. I have been at home yesterday and today.

5. *Tengo muchas maletas y podría prestarte una.* I have many suitcases and could lend you one of them.

6. *Llevaré ropa, zapatos y un sombrero*. I will bring clothes, shoes and a hat.

7. *La escuela para niños y niñas*. The school is for boys and girls.

8. *Estamos felices y muy agradecidos*. We are happy and very grateful.

9. *Comieron y jugaron hasta que se cansaron*. They ate and played until they got tired.

10. *Ustedes y ellos han hecho un gran trabajo.* You and they have done a great job.

Important: In Spanish the letter "H" is silent.

O

The conjunction **"o"** has the meaning of option and it´s used when several possibilities are presented. It is used in the introduction of the last option.

When the word that follows the conjunction begins with **o /ho**, we´ll use **"u"**.

Example:

1. **¿Quieres chocolate o vainilla?** Do you want chocolate or vanilla?
2. **Tenemos deberes u obligaciones**. We have duties or obligations.
3. **¿Te gustaría que tu bebé fuera mujer u hombre?** Would you like your baby to be a woman or a man?
4. **¿Somos amigos o enemigos?** Are we friends or enemies?

5. ***Dime si está claro u oscuro.*** Tell me if it is bright or dark.

6. ***Podemos nadar, cabalgar o escalar.*** We can swim, ride or climb.

7. ***¿Irás a Perú o Ecuador?*** Will you go to Peru or Ecuador?

8. ***Puedes pagar en efectivo o tarjeta de crédito.*** You can pay in cash or credit card.

9. ***¿Vives en el centro de la ciudad o en las afueras?*** Do you live in the center of the city or in the outskirts?

10. ***¿Es un tigre o un león?*** Is it a tiger or a lion?

Shopping

Day 18. Vocabulary & Phrases

Supermercado. Supermarket

Mercado. Market

Librería. Bookstore

Joyería. Jewelry

Centro commercial. Mall

Tienda de ropa. Clothing store

Zapatería. Shoe store

Ropa. Clothing

Zapatos. Shoes

Shorts. Shorts

Camisa / Blusa. Shirt / Blouse

Camiseta. T-Shirt

Falda. Skirt

Pantalón. Pants / Trousers

Corbata. Tie

Traje de baño. Bathing suit

Chinelas. Slippers

Guantes. Gloves

Bufanda. Scarf

Sombrero. Hat

Gorra. Cap

Lentes de sol. Sunglasses

Abrigo. Coat

Calcetines. Socks

Ropa interior. Underwear

Botas. Boots

Reloj. Wristwatch

Rebajas. Sales / Discount

Recibo. Receipt

¿Puedo ayudarte? Can I help you?

Estoy buscando. I am looking for

Vale cinco centavos. It´s cost is five cents.

Está muy caro. It is very expensive.

Está muy barato. It is very cheap.

Muy grande. Too big.

Muy pequeño. Too small.

Más barato Cheaper

Más caro. More expensive.

¿Tienes cambio para diez dólares? Do you have change for ten dollars?

No es mi talla. It´s not my size.

Anillo Ring

Brazalete Bracelet

Cinturón Belt

Collar Necklace

Day 19. Adjectives

The adjectives describe the attributes of a noun and must match the noun in gender and number. They can be male or female, singular or plural, depending on how it finishes.

Example:

1. *La casa es blanca*. The house is white.
2. *Las casas son blancas*. The houses are white.
3. *El bolso es negro*. The bag is black.
4. *Los zapatos son rojos.* The shoes are red.
5. *Tus ojos son hermosos.* Your eyes are beautiful.
6. *Tu mamá es una mujer alta.* Your mom is a tall woman.
7. *Este café está delicioso.* This coffee is delicious.
8. *Juan es un músico famoso.* Juan is a famous musician.
9. *Tus zapatos están sucios.* Your shoes are dirty.
10. *Tu casa es grande y cómoda.* Your house is big and comfortable.

Adjectives are usually placed *after* the noun, only in exceptional situations that they can precede the noun to emphasize the qualities of the noun and their meaning change.

Example:

1. **Un hombre grande.** A big man. (physical quality)
2. **Un gran hombre.** A great man. (personality)
3. **Tu hermano es un buen chico.** Your brother is a good boy.
4. **Tu tío es un hombre bueno.** Your uncle is a good man.
5. **Pasé un mal momento.** I had a bad moment.

*Important: Adjectives **grande, bueno,** and **malo** change according to their location, except the feminine adjectives **buena** and **mala.***

1. **Es una mujer trabajadora.** She is a hard-working woman.
2. **Es un carro pequeño.** It is a small car.
3. **Fue una gran fiesta.** It was a great party.
4. **Fue una fiesta grande.** It was a big party.
5. **Es un hombre casado.** He is a married man.
6. **Soy una persona feliz.** I am a happy person.

7. ***Es una tienda bonita y los artículos son baratos.*** It is a nice store and the items are cheap.

8. ***La torta esta muy dulce.*** The cake is too sweet.

9. ***Este es el carro más lujoso que he visto.*** This is the most luxurious car I have seen.

10. ***Los cachorros son juguetones.*** The puppies are playful.

Day 20. Interrogatives

Interrogatives are used to ask about things, events, or people. In Spanish, every interrogative sentence must have question marks when beginning and ending. They all have an accent.

¿Qué? What? (for things)

¿Cómo? How? (a way, kind or mood)

¿Dónde? Where? (place)

¿Cuándo? When? (time)

¿Cuál? / ¿Cuáles? Which? / What? (people or

things)

¿Quién? / ¿Quiénes? Who? (person)

¿Cuánto/a? / ¿Cuántos/as? How many? (quantity)

¿Por qué? Why? (reason)

Example:

QUÉ

1. ***¿Qué vas a comprar?*** What are you going to buy?
2. ***¿De qué está hecho?*** What is it made of?
3. ***¿De qué color es tu camisa?*** What color is your shirt?
4. ***¿Qué dijo el gerente?*** What did the manager say?
5. ***¿Qué harás mañana?*** What will you do tomorrow?

CÓMO

1. ***¿Cómo es la blusa?*** How is the blouse?

2. **¿Cómo te sientes hoy?** How do you feel today?

3. **¿Cómo preparas la salsa roja?** How do you prepare the red sauce?

4. **¿Cómo es tu familia?** How is your family?

5. **¿Cómo te llamas?** What is your name?

DÓNDE

1. **¿Dónde está la gasolinera?** Where is the gas station?

2. **¿Dónde vive el presidente?** Where does the president live?

3. **¿Dónde está ubicado el Monte Everest?** Where is Mount Everest located?

4. **¿Dónde tomas el autobús?** Where do you take the bus?

5. **¿Dónde trabajas?** Where do you work?

CUÁNDO

1. **¿Cuándo te vas a California?** When are you going to California?

2. **¿Cuándo llegaste a este país?** When did you arrive in this country?

3. **¿Cuándo inicias tus clases?** When do you start your classes?

4. **¿Cuándo vendréis tú y tu familia a visitarme?** When will you and your family come to visit me?

5. **¿Cuándo es la fiesta de graduación?** When is the graduation party?

CUÁL / CUÁLES

1. **¿Cuál es tu canción favorita?** What is your favorite song? (singular)

2. **¿Cuáles son tus planes?** What are your plans? (plural)

3. **¿Cuál es tu número de teléfono?** What is your phone number?

4. **¿Cuáles de estos son tuyos?** Which ones of these are yours?

5. **¿Cuáles son tus expectativas de este trabajo?** What are your expectations of this job?

QUIÉN / QUIÉNES

1. **¿Quién es él?** Who is he? (singular)

2. **¿Quiénes son ellos?** Who are they? (plural)

3. **¿Quién es tu mejor amiga?** Who is your best friend?

4. **¿Quién está en tu casa ahora?** Who is in your house now?

5. **¿Quiénes vendrán a la fiesta?** Who will come to the party?

CUÁNTO/A – CUÁNTOS/AS

1. **¿Cuántas bufandas tienes?** How many scarves do you have?

2. **¿Cuánto cuesta? / ¿Cuánto vale?** How much is it?

3. **¿Cuántos litros de agua hay en este recipiente?** How many liters of water are in this container?

4. **¿Cuántos platos vas a comprar?** How many plates are you going to buy?

5. ***¿Cuántas personas caben en esta sala?*** How many people fit in this room?

POR QUÉ

1. ***¿Por qué estudias Español?*** Why do you study Spanish?
2. ***¿Por qué vendes tu carro?*** Why do you sell your car?
3. ***¿Por qué no irás al cine con tus amigos?*** Why don´t you go to the movie theather with your friends?
4. ***¿Por qué está nevando?*** Why is it snowing?
5. ***¿Por qué esta retrasado el vuelo?*** Why is the flight delayed?

Day 21. There Is / There Are

It´s used to indicate existence or location.

Questions: ***¿Hay*** + subject + complement**?**

¿Hay zapatos de varón? Are there men´s shoes**?**

¿Hay más jugo de manzana? Is there more apple juice?

Affirmative sentences: **Hay** + subject + complement.

Hay muchas piñas en el mercado. There are many pineapples in the market.

Hay muchos niños jugando en el parque. There are many children playing at the park.

Negative sentences: **No hay** + subject + complement.

No hay vino en la licorería. There is no wine in the liquor store.

No hay comida en la despensa. There is no food in the pantry.

Examples:

1. **Hay muchos turistas comprando hoy**. There are many tourists buying today.

2. **_No hay cambio en la caja._** There is no change in the box.

3. **_¿Hay algo que comprar?_** Is there something to buy?

4. **_¿Hay leche en la lechería?_** Is there milk in the dairy?

5. **_Hay un hermoso arcoiris en el cielo._** There is a beautiful rainbow in the sky.

6. **_Hay chocolates dentro de ese recipiente azul._** There are chocolates inside that blue container.

7. **_Hay una gran fila para comprar._** There is a large queue to buy.

8. **_¿Hay alguien que puede ayudarme?_** Is there someone who can help me?

9. **_No hay agua en el tanque._** There is no water in the tank.

10. **_Hay muchos alumnos en la clase de español._** There are many students in the Spanish class.

Money

Day 22. Vocabulary & Phrases

Dinero Money / Bill

Monedas Coins

Divisa / Moneda nacional Currency

Efectivo Cash

Propina Tip

Pagar Pay

Pago Payment

Tarjeta de crédito Credit card

Tarjeta de débito Debit card

Cuenta bancaria Bank account

Préstamo Loan

Factura Invoice

Gratis Free

Descuento Discount

Insolvente / Banca rota Bankrupt

Deuda Debt

Cheque Check

Cuenta corriente Checking account

Cuenta de ahorros Savings account

Prestamista Moneylender

Ahorrar Save

Gastar Spend

Ganar dinero Earn money

Sueldo / Salario Salary / Wage

Cobrar Get paid

Rico / Adinerado Wealthy

¿Podrías prestarme? Could you lend me?

Tipo de cambio Exchange rate

Cajero automático ATM

Pedir prestado To borrow

Dar prestado To lend

Day 23. Simple Conditional

It´s used to express wishes, courtesy, give advice and suggestions. In English, we use "would" to conjugate the verb to simple conditional and the conjugation of verbs in Spanish is different. You should conjugate verbs using endings like *ía, ías, íamos, and ían*.

Add these endings to the infinitive verb:

Infinitive Verb + ía/ías/íamos/ían.

Comprar Buy

Yo compraría I would buy

Tú comprarías You would buy

El / Ella compraría He / She would buy

Nosotros compraríamos We would buy

Ustedes comprarían You would buy

Ellos comprarían They would buy

Reir (to laugh), **comer** (to eat), **amar** (to love), *odiar* (to hate), *sentir* (to feel), *caer* (to fall) are some regular Spanish verbs.

Terminations are the same, regardless of whether the infinitive ends in *ar, er, ir*.

Irregular Spanish Verbs & conjugation 1st person, singular

Salir Leave Sal**dr**ía

Tener Have Ten**dr**ía

Valer Worth Val**dr**ía

Querer Want Que**rr**ía

Decir Say **Dir**ía

Hacer Make **Har**ía

Poner Put Pon**dr**ía

Poder Be able to Po**dr**ía

Saber Know Sa**br**ía

Haber Have Ha**br**ía

Caber Fit Ca**br**ía

Venir Come Ven**dría**

Important: Conjugation for irregular Spanish verbs is different from the regular´s. The endings do not differ with respect to irregular verbs, it is the verb per se that suffer a modification.

<u>Examples:</u>

1. ***Me gustaría abrir una cuenta de ahorros.*** I would like to open a savings account.
2. ***Ustedes deberían pagar su deuda.*** You should pay your debt.
3. ***Valdría la pena gastar mis ahorros en París***. It would be worth spending my savings in Paris.
4. ***Ganaría mucho más.*** I would earn much more.
5. ***No tendrías propina***. You would not have a tip.
6. ***Saldría todos los días a comer a mi restaurante favorito***. I would go out everyday to eat at my favourite restaurant.

7. ***Si estuviera contigo querría abrazarte***. If I were with you, I would like to hold you.

8. ***Si fuera un secreto no lo diríamos.*** If it was a secret, we would not say it.

9. ***Ellos harían lo necesario por tí.*** They would do what is necessary for you.

10. ***Con mucho dinero pondríamos un gran restaurante.*** With a lot of money, we would put a great restaurant.

Time And Date

Day 24. Vocabulary & Phrases

Hora y Fecha. Time and date

Hoy. Today

Ayer. Yesterday

Anteayer / Antier. Before yesterday

Mañana. Tomorrow

Pasado mañana. Day after tomorrow

Horas Hours

Minutos Minutes

Segundos Seconds

Días Days

Semana Week

Fin de semana. Weekend

Meses Months

Años Years

Hace muchos años. Many years ago

Cita Appointment

¿Qué hora es? What time is it?

Es temprano. It´s early.

Es muy tarde. It´s too late.

Estás retrasado. You are late.

En los años 90s (noventas). In the 90s.

¿Qué fecha es hoy? What date is today?

¿Que día es hoy? What day is today?

¿Hace cuánto tiempo? How long ago?

Day 25. Holidays

Feriado. Holiday

Vacaciones. Holidays

Año Nuevo. New Year

Víspera de año Nuevo. New Year´s Eve

Día de los muertos. Day of the Dead

Navidad. Christmas

Feliz navidad. Merry Christmas

Día de San Valentín Valentine´s Day

Aniversario Anniversary

Semana Santa Easter Week

Días de la semana. Days of the week

Lunes. Monday

Martes.Tuesday

Miércoles. Wednesday

Jueves. Thursday

Viernes. Friday

Sábado. Saturday

Domingo. Sunday

Enero January

Febrero February

Marzo March

Abril April

Mayo May

Junio June

Julio July

Agosto August

Septiembre September

Octubre October

Noviembre November

Diciembre December

Day 26. Present Simple

Present simple or indicative present is used to talk about actions that occur in the moment or immediate future. To describe repeated actions, or routine, facts that do not change, or real situations.

To conjugate, you should eliminate the ending of infinitive like *ar, er, ir*, then add the proper form according to each person (singular & plural).

Hablar.

Yo hablo. I speak

Tú hablas. You speak

Él / Ella habla. He / She speaks

Nosotros hablamos. We speak

Ustedes hablan. You speak

Ellos hablan. They speak

Prestar

Yo presto. I lend

Tú prestas. You lend

Él / Ella presta. He / She lends

Nosotros prestamos. We lend

Ustedes prestan. You lend

Ellos prestan. They lend

Example:

1. *Ahorrar: Todos los días ahorro cinco dólares.* Everyday I save five dollars.

2. **Tener: Tengo este trabajo desde el 2011.** I have this job since 2011.

3. **Vivir: El presindente de los Estados Unidos vive en la Casa Blanca.** The President of the United States lives in the White House.

4. **Cerrar: El banco cierra a las 2 pm.** The bank closes at 2 pm.

5. **Caer: Todos los días caen muchas naranjas del árbol.** Everyday many oranges fall from the tree.

6. **Amar: Yo sé que amas mucho a tu hijo**. I know that you love your child very much.

7. **Hablar: Ella habla español muy bien.** She speaks Spanish very well.

8. **Manejar: Nosotros manejamos el mismo carro.** We drive the same car.

9. **Comer: Ustedes comen muy rápido.** You eat very fast.

10. **Escribir: Escribimos cartas todas las noches.** We write letters every night.

Important: Some verbs are irregular and you should

*add a **"g"** between the root and the ending in first singular person. Sometimes the root of the word must be modified.*

Example:

Caer

Yo caigo. I fall

1. *Si caigo, me levanto*. If I fall, I get up.
2. *Si caigo al suelo me golpearé*. If I fall to the ground, I will hit myself.

Decir

Yo digo. I say

1. *Yo digo que sí.* I say yes.
2. *Si digo una mentira, no confiarán en mí.* If I tell a lie, they will not trust me.

Hacer

Yo hago. I make

1. *Yo hago el cierre de ventas todos los sábados.* I make the closing sales every Saturday.
2. *Cuando hago una comida, a todos les gusta.* When I make a meal, everyone likes it.

Day 27. Past Simple

Past simple or preterite tense forms are used to describe actions *completed* in the past. To conjugate regular verbs in the past tense, remove the ending *ar, er, ir* and add the ending that matches the subject.

Verbs that end in **ar**

Amar

Yo amé. I loved

Tú amaste. You loved

El / Ella amó. He / She loved

Nosotros amamos. We loved

Ustedes amaron. You loved

Ellos amaron. They loved

Verbs that end in **er, ir**

Comer

Yo comí. I ate

Tú comiste. You ate

El / Ella comió. He / She ate

Nosotros comimos. We ate

Ustedes comieron. Yoy ate

Ellos comieron. They ate

Pedir

Yo pedí. I asked

Tú pediste. You asked

El / Ella pidió. He / She asked

Nosotros pedimos. We asked

Ustedes pidieron. You asked

Ellos pidieron. They asked

Example:

1. **Prestar. Mi banco me prestó un millón de euros.** My bank lent me one million euros.

2. **Salir. Salimos a cenar el domingo pasado.** We went out for dinner last Sunday.

3. **Disfrutar. Disfruté el fin de semana.** I enjoyed the weekend.

4. **Cantar. Cantó en el concierto de rock el año pasado.** She sang at the rock concert last year.

5. **Ser. Fuimos novios hace mucho tiempo.** We were boyfriends a long time ago.

6. **Ser. El accidente fue grave, eran las diez de la noche**. The accident was serious, it was ten o´clock at night.

7. **Caer. Nos caímos de la bicicleta.** We fell off the bike.

8. **Hacer. Los niños hicieron una buena presentación.** The children made a good presentation.

9. **Dormir. Juan durmió toda la tarde.** Juan slept all afternoon.

10. *Estudiar. Ayer estudié mi lección de español.* I studied my Spanish lesson yesterday.

Day 28. Verb *Estar* In Past Simple

Verb **"estar"** has an irregular verbal conjugation.

1. Imperfect Tense Form:

   It is used to describe a past situation, past routines or actions that were done frequently, an action that was in progress when another action interrupted it.

   Yo estaba I was

   Tú estabas You were

   Él / Ella estaba He / She was

   Nosotros estábamos We were

   Ustedes estaban You were

   Ellos / Ellas estaban They were

   Example:

1. ***Javier estaba en la misma área que yo.*** Javier was in the same area as me. (A past situation)

2. ***Cuando yo era una niña, estaba muy delgada.*** When I was a child, I was very thin. (A past state)

3. ***Ellos estaban en el centro comercial cuando le robaron el teléfono.*** They were in the mall when his phone was stolen. (Action in progress when another action interrupted it)

2. Simple Past Tense:

It applies to actions completed in the past that are not related to a present situation, facts in the past or an action that interrupts another.

Yo estuve I was

Tú estuviste You were

Él / Ella estuvo He / She was

Nosotros estuvimos We were

Ustedes estuvieron You were

Ellos/Ellas estuvieron They were

Example:

1. **El año pasado estuve en un curso de Francés.** Last year I was in a French course. (An action completed in the past)

2. **Ella estuvo en el lugar del accidente.** She was at the accident scene. (Fact in the past)

3. **Te dieron vacaciones por que estuviste enfermo.** They gave you vacation because you were sick.

Day 29. Future Simple

Future simple is used to express that an action will occur after a present or past moment, future also expresses probability and possibility.

Hablar

Yo hablaré. I will speak

Tú hablarás. You will speak

Él / Ella hablará. He / She speak

Nosotros hablaremos. We will speak

Ustedes hablarán. You will speak

Ellos hablarán. They will speak

Ser

Yo seré. I will be

Tú serás. You will be

Él / Ella Será. He / She will be

Nosotros seremos. We will be

Ustedes serán. You will be

Ellos serán. They will be

Estar

Yo estaré. I will be

Tú estarás. You will be

Él / Ella estará. He / She will be

Nosotros estaremos. We will be

Ustedes estarán. You will be

Ellos estarán. They will be

Example:

1. ***Hablaré con su asistente para programar una cita****. I will talk to his assistant to set an appointment.
2. ***Cocinaremos pasta para cenar****. We will cook pasta for dinner.
3. ***Ellos estarán contentos de verte****. They will be happy to see you.
4. ***¿Vendrán a visitarnos?*** Will you come to visit us?
5. ***Bob saldrá a las 9 am de la mañana****. Bob will leave at 9 in the morning.
6. ***Iremos a acampar la próxima semana.*** We will go camping next week.
7. ***Los novios irán de luna de miel a Dubai****. The couple will go on their honeymoon to Dubai.
8. ***Estudiaré para ser abogada****. I will study to be a lawyer.

9. ***Los niños cantarán en el festival el próximo martes.*** The children will sing at the festival next Tuesday.

10. ***Estaré fuera del país durante dos años***. I will be out of the country for two years.

Family

Day 30. Vocabulary

Familia Family

Mamá Mom

Madre Mother

Papá Dad

Padre Father

Hijo Son

Hija Daughter

Hermano Brother

Hermana Sister

Hermanos carnales Siblings

Padres Parents

Abuelo Grandfather

Abuela Grandmother

Nieto Grandson

Nieta Granddaughter

Niños Kids / Children

Tío Uncle

Tía Aunt

Sobrino Nephew

Sobrina Niece

Primo/a Cousin

Cuñado Brother-in-Law

Cuñada Sister-in-Law

Suegro Father-in-Law

Suegra Mother-in-Law

Yerno Son-in-Law

Nuera Daughter-in-Law

Esposo Husband

Esposa Wife

Hogar Home

Casa House

Bisnieto Great-grandson

Bisnieta Great-granddaughter

Day 31. Gerund

A gerund is a non-personal form of the verb. Sometimes gerunds are exclamatory phrases or indicate order and they are not accompanied by the main verb, for example *¡Circulando!* Or *¡Andando!*

Gerund must follow three conditions: that works as an adverb or as a verb; which express a simultaneous action or previous to that of the main verb; and the subject of the gerund must be the same as that of the main verb. In Spanish, use *ando, iendo, endo, yendo* to congugate the verb.

Example:

1. *Me gusta escuchar música mientras estoy cocinando.* I like to listen to music while I am cooking.

2. ***Los vimos jugando fútbol.*** We saw them playing soccer.

3. ***Se quemó con agua hirviendo***. She burned herself with boiling water.

4. ***¿Qué estás haciendo?*** What are you doing?

5. ***Estoy viendo televisión.*** I am watching TV.

6. ***Terminando de estudiar, iremos a surfear***. When we finish studying, we will go surfing.

7. ***Estoy saliendo con tu hermana.*** I am dating your sister.

8. ***Debes tocar el piano siguiendo las instrucciones de tu maestro***. You should play the piano following the instructions of your teacher.

9. ***No puedo hablar porque estoy conduciendo.*** I cannot talk because I am driving.

10. ***Los chicos están bailando.*** The boys are dancing.

Day 32. Present Progressive

Present progressive or continuous is used to talk about actions that are happening at the moment. The grammar structure for present progressive is the verb to be *(estar)* in the present tense and the verb in gerund (present participle).

To be *(estar)* + *Gerund*

Add the termination *–ando* to form the gerund for verbs that end in *ar.* Add *–iendo* for verbs ending in *er, ir*.

Estudiar Study

Yo estoy estudiando. I am studying.

Tú estás estudiando. You are studying.

Él / Ella está estudiando. He / She is studying.

Nosotros estamos estudiando. We are studying.

Ustedes están estudiando. You are studying.

Ellos/Ellas están estudiando. They are studying.

Comer Eat

Yo estoy comiendo. I am eating.

Tú estás comiendo. You are eating.

Él / Ella está comiendo. He / She is eating.

Nosotros estamos comiendo. We are eating.

Ustedes están comiendo. You are eating.

Ellos / Ellas están comiendo. They are eating.

Dormir Sleep

Yo estoy durmiendo. I am sleeping.

Tú estás durmiendo. You are sleeping.

Él / Ella está durmiendo. He / She is sleeping.

Nosotros estamos durmiendo. We are sleeping.

Ustedes están durmiendo. You are sleeping.

Ellos/Ellas están durmiendo. They are sleeping.

Example:

1. ***Las gimnastas están practicando para el torneo.*** The gymnasts are practicing for the tournament.

2. **_Estoy disfrutando del paseo en este lugar hermoso._** I am enjoying the walk in this beautiful place.

3. **_Está lloviendo tan fuerte que puedo escuchar las gotas sobre el tejado._** It is raining so hard that I can hear the drops on the roof.

4. **_Mis papás están visitando a mis abuelos en Canadá._** My parents are visiting my grandparents in Canada.

5. **_No puedo contestar el teléfono porque estoy lavando los platos._** I cannot answer the phone because I am washing the dishes.

6. **_Aún estamos esperando en la clínica porque el doctor no llega._** We are still waiting at the clinic because the doctor does not arrive.

7. **_Estamos viajando hacia Perú._** We are traveling to Peru.

8. **_No puedo creer lo que está sucediendo ahora mismo._** I cannot believe what is happening right now.

9. **_Ellos están corriendo en el campo._** They are running in the field.

10. *Estamos cantando la misma canción.* We are singing the same song.

Day 33. Past Progressive

Past progressive or past continuous is used to talk about an action that was happening in the past. The grammar structure for past progressive is verb to be *"estar"* in the past tense and the verb in gerund (present participle).

Esperar Wait

Yo estaba esperando. I was waiting.

Tú estabas esperando. You were waiting.

Él/ Ella estaba esperando. He / She was waiting.

Nosotros estábamos esperando. We were waiting.

Ustedes estaban esperando. You were waiting.

Ellos estaban esperando. They were waiting.

__Hacer__ Do

__Yo estaba haciendo.__ I was doing.

__Tú estabas haciendo.__ You were doing.

__Él / Ella estaba haciendo.__ He / She was doing.

__Nosotros estábamos haciendo.__ We were doing.

__Ustedes estaban haciendo.__ You were doing.

__Ellos estaban haciendo.__ They were doing.

__Mentir__ Lie

__Yo estaba mintiendo.__ I was lying.

__Tú estabas mintiendo.__ You were lying.

__Él / Ella estaba mintiendo.__ He / She was lying.

__Nosotros estábamos mintiendo.__ We were lying.

__Ustedes estaban mintiendo.__ You were lying.

__Ellos estaban mintiendo.__ They were lying.

Example:

1. ***Él estaba ganando mucho dinero en aquel trabajo.*** He was making a lot of money in that job.

2. ***Estaba estudiando para mi examen de español cuando recibí tu mensaje.*** I was studying for my Spanish exam when I received your message.

3. ***Ellos estaban viendo la película de Star Wars.*** They were watching the Star Wars movie.

4. ***Estábamos comiendo todos juntos cuando recibimos la noticia.*** We were all eating together when we received the news.

5. ***Ella estaba durmiendo mientras yo leía.*** She was sleeping while I was reading.

6. ***Ayer estábamos jugando al tenis en tu casa.*** Yesterday we were playing tennis at your home.

7. ***Los niños estaban jugando en el jardín cuando su mamá vino a buscarlos.*** The children were playing in the garden when their mom came for them.

8. ***Ellos estaban hablando sobre un asunto importante.*** They were talking about an important issue.

9. ***Todos estaban haciendo lo mismo.*** Everyone was doing the same.

10. ***Estábamos estudiando juntos el año pasado en la misma escuela.*** We were studying together at the same school last year.

Home

Day 34. Vocabulary.

Sala Living room

Comedor Dining room

Jardín Garden

Patio Yard

Garaje Garage

Terraza Terrace

Dormitorio / Habitación Bedroom

Baño Bathroom

Ducha Shower

Toalla Towel

Segundo piso Upstairs

Planta baja Downstairs

Cocina Kitchen

Cafetera Coffee maker

Licuadora Blender

Biblioteca Library

Estante para libros Bookshelf

Oficina Office

Escritorio Desk

Televisor TV

Cama Bed

Armario Closet

Mesa de noche Nightstand

Lámpara Lamp

Cortinas Courtains

Sofá Sofa

Mesa Table

Muebles Furniture

Platos Plates

Cuchara Spoon

Cucharita Teaspoon

Tenedor Fork

Cuchillo Knife

Servilleta Napkin

Vaso Glass

Reloj Clock

Ventana Window

Puerta Door

Techo / Tejado Ceiling

Piso Floor

Alfombra Carpet / Rug

Computadora Computer

Lampazo / Trapeador Mop

Aspiradora Vacuum Cleaner

Day 35. Demonstrative Pronouns I

Demonstrative pronouns are used to indicate a person, animal or thing. They allow indicating the distance with respect to the speaker.

Aquel / Aquella-s / Aquellos:

Are used to show the distance between the object and the speaker or listener.

There are two singulars: *aquel* (masculine) and *aquella* (feminine). And two plurals: *aquellos* (masculine) and *aquellas* (feminine).

Example:

1. *Me gusta aquella mochila.* I like that backpack.
2. *Los libros están en aquel armario.* The books are on that closet.
3. *Aquellos mangos se ven deliciosos.* Those mangos look delicious.
4. *¿Recuerdas aquellas niñas que vimos en el restaurante?* Do you remember those girls that we saw at the restaurant?
5. *Aquellos hombres trabajan para mi empresa.* Those men work for my company.
6. *La tienda está ubicada donde está aquel rótulo.* The store is located where that lettering is.

7. *Me gusta aquel cuadro que tienes en la pared.* I like that painting you have on the wall.

8. *¿Conoces a aquella joven?* Do you know that young woman?

9. *Aquel señor es socio de mi padre.* That gentleman is a partner of my father.

10. *Aquellas son mis faldas.* Those are my skirts.

More Examples:

1. *Aquel vaso está roto, deberías botarlo.* That glass is broken, you should throw it away. (masculine/singular)

2. *Aquellas frutas se ven limpias y frescas.* Those fruits look clean and fresh. (feminine/plural)

3. *Aquellos platos están sucios.* Those plates are dirty. (masculine/plural)

4. *Aquel árbol es de madera preciosa.* That tree is made of precious wood. (masculine/singular)

5. *Aquellas plantas son medicinales.* Those plants are medicinal. (feminine/plural)

6. *Aquella luz es muy intensa, por favor apágala.* That light is very intense, please turn it off. (feminine/singular)

7. *Aquella mujer es la dueña de la escuela.* That woman is the owner of the school. (feminine/singular)

Day 36. Demonstrative Pronouns II

Este / Esta / Esto-s / Esta-s

These demonstrative pronouns are used to describe something close to the speaker or listener, either in the time (recently) or at space (close).

Este, Esto, Estos *(plural)* are used for masculine nouns. *Esta, Estas* *(plural)* are used for feminine nouns.

Example:

1. *Este regalo es para tí*. This gift is for you.

2. *Esta es la mía*. This is mine.

3. *Estos son tus cuadernos*. These are your notebooks.

4. *¿De quién es esto?* Whose is this?

5. *Te doy estas monedas*. I give you these coins.

6. *Esta taza de té es para tí*. This cup of tea is for you.

7. *Estos niños son excelentes estudiantes*. These children are excellent students.

8. *Estas copas son las mías*. These glasses are mine.

9. *¿Son estos mis lentes?* Are these my glasses?

10. *Este banco es el más grande de la región.* This bank is the biggest of the region.

More Examples:

1. *Esta silla es muy suave.* This chair is very soft.

2. *Esta mesa amarilla es de plástico.* This yellow table is made of plastic.

3. *Estas alfombras son de piel.* These carpets are made of leather.

4. ***Estos vasos son una vasija fina.*** These glasses are a glassware.

5. ***Estas camas son demasiado pequeñas.*** These beds are too small.

6. ***Este libro es una autobiografía.*** This book is an autobiography.

7. ***Este televisor es de 14 pulgadas.*** This TV is 14 inches.

Day 37. Demonstrative Pronouns III

Ese / Esa-s / Esos

These demonstrative pronouns are used when you are talking about something that you can see or something close to the listener, but you can not reach or touch.

Ese, Esos *(plural)* are used for masculine nouns, and ***Esa, Esas*** *(plural)* are used for feminine nouns.

Example:

1. **¿Vendes esas cortinas?** Do you sell those curtains?

2. **Por favor, dame ese lápiz**. Please, give me that pencil.

3. **Esas flores están lindas**. Those flowers are beautiful.

4. **Esos perros son bravos**. Those dogs are wild.

5. **Esos aretes estan bonitos**. Those earrings are pretty.

6. **En este zoológico cuidan bien a esos animales.** In this zoo they take good care of those animals.

7. **Esas pitahayas se ven deliciosas.** Those dragon fruits look delicious.

8. **Por favor, pásame esa botella.** Please, pass me that bottle.

9. **Recuerdo que usaste ese traje el día de tu boda**. I remember you wore that suit on your wedding day.

10. **Esas son mis medicinas**. Those are my medicines.

More Examples:

1. *Ese hombre estuvo en nuestra casa ayer.* That man was in our house yesterday.

2. *Me gusta ese sombrero marrón.* I like that brown hat.

3. *Esa papelera está dañada.* That bin is damaged.

4. *Esos anillos son los de nuestra boda.* Those rings are the ones from our wedding.

5. *Esas computadoras son nuevas.* Those computers are new.

6. *Esas escaleras se ven peligrosas.* Those leaders look dangerous.

7. *Esas almohadas se ven tan suaves.* Those pillows look so soft.

Food

Day 38. Vocabulary

Frutas Fruits

Verduras / Vegetales Vegetables

Carne Meat

Cerdo Pork

Res Beef

Pescado Fish

Pollo Chicken

Pavo Turkey

Desayuno Breakfast

Almuerzo Lunch

Cena Dinner

Merienda Snack

Cocinar To cook

Galletas Cookies

Leche Milk

Sopa Soup

Arroz Rice

Frijoles Beans

Cerveza Beer

Vino Wine

Agua mineral Mineral water

Agua Water

Gaseosa / Soda Soda

Mantequilla Butter

Jalea Jelly

Pan Bread

Aceite Oil

Aceite de oliva Olive oil

Estufa Stove

Mantequilla de maní Peanut butter

Pastel Cake

Postre Dessert

Ensalada Salad

Dulce Sweet

Ácido Sour

Amargo Bitter

Salado Salty

Picante Spicy

Papa Potato

Lechuga Lettuce

Cebolla Onion

Ajo Garlic

Rábano Radish

Apio Celery

Romero Rosemary

Delicioso Delicious

Soy vegetarian. I am vegetarian.

Me gustaría ordenar. I would like to order.

¿Qué me recomiendas comer? What do you recommend me to eat?

No me gusta. I don´t like it.

Sal Salt

Pimienta Pepper

Horno Oven

Refrigerador Fridge

Está congelado. It is frozen.

Day 39. To Like (Gustar)

It is a special verb in Spanish because the subject personal pronoun is not used. Instead, you must use indirect object pronouns. **Gustar** is only conjugated in the *third person singular and plural* (**Gusta or Gustan** in Present)

Indirect Object Pronouns

Yo = Me

Tú = Te

Él / Ella = Le

Nosotros = Nos

Ustedes = Les

Ellos = Les

Sentence: *IO Pronoun* + ***Gusta / Gustan*** + *Complement*

Singular or plural? Use singular when there is a *singular noun after* the verb, and it must always be accompanied by a definite article. When there is an *infinitive verb after* **gusta** you should use the *singular form*.

Example:

1. ***Me gusta el pollo con vegetales***. I like chicken with vegetables.
2. ***Nos gusta comer verduras al menos una vez a la semana.*** We like to eat vegetables at least once a week.
3. ***Les gusta desayunar tarde***. They like to have breakfast late.

4. *Me gusta hacer pasteles para mis nietos*. I like to make cakes for my grandchildren.

5. *Le gusta cocinar comida china.* He likes to cook Chinese food.

6. *¿Te gusta el jugo de pera?* Do you like pear juice?

7. *Te gusta la sopa de mariscos, la prepararé para ti.* You like seafood soup; I will prepare it for you.

8. *Me gusta compartir con mis amigos.* I like to share with my friends.

9. *Les gusta ir de compras juntos.* They like to go shopping together.

10. *Le gusta ver televisión mientras come.* He likes to watch TV while he eats.

Use the plural form when there is a *plural noun after* the verb *gustan, or* when you list different nouns.

Example:

1. *Nos gustan las frutas con cereal.* We like fruits with cereal.

2. *Le gustan el pollo y el cerdo, pero no le gusta el pescado.* He likes chicken and pork, but he doesn´t like fish.

3. *Me gustan las galletas saladas.* I like salty cookies.

4. *Les gustan las papas.* They like potatoes.

5. *Nos gustan los chocolates.* We like chocolates.

6. *No me gustan las bebidas calientes.* I do not like hot drinks.

7. *Me gustan el arroz, las lentejas y los garbanzos.* I like rice, lentils, and chickpeas.

8. *Me gustan los helados de papaya, es mi fruta favorita.* I like papaya ice cream, it´s my favorite fruit.

9. *¿Les gustan las hamburguesas de pollo?* Do you like chicken burgers?

10. *Me gustan los restaurantes de comida rápida.* I like fast food restaurants.

Important: When there are several infinitive verbs

after the verb gustar, use the singular form.

Example:

1. ***Te gusta cantar, bailar y escribir***. You like to sing, dance, and write.

2. ***Le gusta cocinar, planchar y arreglar el jardín***. She likes to cook, iron, and tidy up the garden.

3. ***Les gusta escuchar música y ver películas en español***. They like to listen to music and watch movies in Spanish.

4. ***Le gusta escribir y publicar libros para niños***. He likes to write and publish books for children.

5. ***Me gusta leer, escribir y componer artículos sobre medicina***. I like to read, write, and compose articles about medicine.

6. ***Nos gusta hacer ejercicios todas las mañanas.*** We like to do exercises every morning.

7. ***Le gusta hablar contigo porque eres muy amable***. She likes to talk to you because you are very kind.

8. **Me gusta trabajar y administrar mi propio dinero.** I like to work and manage my own money.

9. **Te gusta ver las noticias nacionales todas las noches.** You like to watch national news every night.

10. **Les gusta viajar y comprar cosas**. They like to travel and buy things.

Day 40. Definite & Indefinite Articles

Articles are words that define a noun. In Spanish, an article is determined by the gender of the noun.

Definite Articles are used to talk about something known or that you can identify. *Definite masculine* articles are **el** (singular) and **los** (plural). *Definite feminine* articles are **la** (singular) and **las** (plural).

Example:

1. **Me gustan los frijoles rojos.** I like red beans.

2. **Por favor, sírvete la ensalada.** Please, serve the salad for yourself.

3. **Las cebollas están frescas.** The onions are fresh.

4. **El pepino está muy barato**. The cucumber is very cheap.

5. **La cerveza está muy fría**. The beer is very cold.

6. **Los tomates están muy baratos.** The tomatoes are very cheap.

7. **El ajo tiene propiedades medicinales.** Garlic has medicinal properties.

8. **Las uvas verdes son mis favoritas.** Green grapes are my favorites.

9. **La comida está servida en la mesa**. The food is served on the table.

10. **Los niños comen muchos dulces**. Children eat lots of sweets.

Indefinite articles are used to refer to something undefined or unspecified, they are used *after* the word **hay** (There is / There are). *Indefinite masculine* articles are **un** (singular) and **unos** (plural).

Indefinite feminine articles are **una** (singular) and **unas** (plural).

Example:

1. **Hay un libro de español en tu mesa.** There is a Spanish book on your table.

2. **Compré unas piñas para el desayuno**. I bought some pineapples for breakfast.

3. **Iré con una amiga al mercado de pescado.** I´ll go with a friend to the fish market.

4. **Traje unas frutas para tu asistente**. I brought some fruits for your assistant.

5. **Tengo unos frijoles que están en una lata.** I have some beans that are in a can.

6. **Hay un pepino en el refrigerador.** There is a cucumber in the fridge.

7. **Hay unos helados muy ricos que preparó mi mamá.** There are some very delicious ice creams that my mom prepared.

8. **Esto es un regalo que me dio mi suegra.** This is a gift that my mother-in-law gave me.

9. **Quiero una mascota.** I want a pet.

10. ***Estamos en un dilema.*** We are in a dilemma.

Weather

Day 41. Vocabulary

Clima Weather

Temperatura Temperature

Estación Season

Invierno Winter

Verano Summer

Primavera Spring

Otoño Autumn

Frío Cold

Caliente Hot

Húmedo Humid / Wet

Ventoso Windy

Nublado Cloudy

Soleado Sunny

Lluvia Rain

Nieve Snow

Está nevando It´s snowing

Está lluvioso It´s rainy

Sombrilla / Paragüa Umbrella

Bloqueador solar Sun Block

Grados Celsius Degrees Celcius

Grados Fahrenheit Degrees Fahrenheit

Tormenta Storm

Huracán Hurricane

Maremoto Seaquake

Terremoto Earthquake

Inundación Flood

Avalancha Snowslide

Tormenta eléctrica Electric Storm

Relámpagos Lightning bolts

¿Cuál es la temperatura hoy? What´s the temperature today?

Hoy estará lloviendo. Today will be raining.

Mañana será un día soleado. Tomorrow will be a

sunny day.

La temperatura bajará. The temperature will decrease.

Dos grados bajo cero Two degrees under zero

¿Cuál es el pronóstico del tiempo para hoy? What is the weather forecast for today?

El día está despejado. The day is clear.

Tengo mucho frío. I am very cold.

Day 42. Muchos / Mucho Vs Muy

Muy is an adverb that means *very* in English. It has no masculine or feminine and no plural or singular form either. You can use **muy** before an adjective to increase or highlight its intensity. You can also use **muy** before an adverb, but never use the word by itself.

Example:

1. **Hoy está muy nublado**. Today is very cloudy.

2. ***Este bloqueador es muy bueno***. This sunblock is very good.

3. ***La sombrilla es muy pequeña***. The umbrella is very small.

4. ***El clima es muy húmedo y caliente***. The weather is very humid and hot.

5. ***Este abrigo está muy grande, necesito uno más pequeño.*** This coat is very big, I need a smaller one.

6. ***El cielo está muy claro hoy, es un buen día para salir.*** The sky is very clear today, it´s a good day to go out.

7. ***Estoy muy feliz de verte.*** I am very happy to see you.

8. ***La Primera Guerra Mundial fue muy cruel.*** The First World War was very cruel.

9. ***El pronóstico del tiempo no es muy favorable.*** The weather forecast is not very favorable.

10. ***Necesitan estar muy abrigados para soportar el frío.*** You need to be very warm to withstand the cold.

Mucho/s can be used as an adverb or as an adjective, for *masculine nouns* you must use the form **mucho / muchos**, and for *feminine nouns* use **mucha / muchas**. It usually goes before a noun.

Example:

1. **Mi hermana tiene muchas amigas.** My sister has many friends.
2. **Hace mucho calor en el desierto de Atacama.** It is very hot in the Atacama Desert.
3. **No quiero salir de casa, tengo mucho frío.** I don´t want to leave the house, I am very cold.
4. **Hay muchas casas en este residencial.** There are many houses in this residential.
5. **Te quiero mucho y lo sabes.** I love you so much and you know it.
6. **Me gustaría tener mucho dinero para ayudar a los pobres.** I´d like to have a lot of money to help poor people.

7. **Tengo mucha hambre, compraré algo para llevar.** I am very hungry; I will buy something to carry.

8. **Tienes muchas mascotas en tu casa, te gustan los animales.** You have many pets in your house, you like animals.

9. **Hemos conocido muchas personas en nuestros viajes.** We have met many people in our trips.

10. **Me dio mucho gusto trabajar contigo en este proyecto.** I was very happy to work with you on this project.

Sometimes it´s used as an adverb and goes after the verb, in this specific case you´ll always use the same form **mucho.**

Example:

1. **Ayer nevó mucho durante la noche**. It snowed a lot yesterday at night.

2. *Mi esposo trabaja mucho*. My husband works a lot.

3. *Las pastas me gustan mucho.* I like pasta a lot.

4. *La comida estaba deliciosa y comí mucho.* The food was delicious and I ate a lot.

5. *La herida está sangrando mucho*. The wound is bleeding a lot.

6. *Disfruté mucho el paseo a la playa*. I enjoyed a lot the walk to the beach.

7. *Has cambiado mucho, pero para bien*. You have changed a lot, but for the better.

8. *Los niños jugaron mucho tiempo en la playa y están cansados*. The children played a lot of time on the beach and they are tired.

9. *Dormí mucho ayer*. I slept a lot yesterday.

10. *La moneda cambió mucho el año pasado*. The currency changed a lot last year.

Hobbies

Day 43. Vocabulary

Pasa tiempo Hobby

Tiempo libre Free time

Salir To go out

Bailar To dance

Cocinar To cook

Cantar To sing

Viajar To travel

Tocar el piano To play the piano

Tocar la guitarra To play the guitar

Escuchar música To listen to music

Leer To read

Escribir To write

Navegar en internet To surf the net

Redes sociales Social networks

Fotografía Photography

Trabajar To work

Ir al mar Go to the beach

Nadar To swim

Acampar To camp

Hacer ejercicios To do exercises

Montar a caballo To ride a horse

Andar en bicicleta To ride a bike

Caminar To walk

Visitar a mis amigos To visit my friends

Escalar To climb

Hacer Kayac Kayak

Senderismo Trekking

Bucear Diving / Snorkeling

Patinar Skate / Rollerblading

Esquiar To ski

Surfear To Surf

Estudiar Español To study Spanish

Pintar To paint

Patinar sobre hielo Ice skating

Ir de compras To go shopping

¿Cuál es tu pasatiempo favorito? What is your favorite pastime?

¿Qué haces en tu tiempo libre? What do you do in your free time?

Me gusta. I like.

Day 44. Comparatives

To compare people and animals and highlight the most relevant of these. The verb is implicit and shouldn´t be repeated since it appears in the first element of the sentence.

Inequality: Difference in quality or value between the two elements.

Más / menos + *Adjective/Noun/Adverb* + *que*

When the comparative is followed by a *number*, it´s used *más / menos de.*

Example:

1. ***Mi papá es <u>más alto que</u> mi mamá***. My dad is taller than my mom.

2. ***Yo cocino <u>más rápido que</u> mi hermana.*** I cook faster than my sister.

3. ***Mi esposa tiene <u>menos amigos que</u> yo***. My wife has less friends than me.

4. ***Mi primo me prestó <u>más de</u> mil dólares***. My cousin lent me more than a thousand dollars.

5. ***Peso un kilogramo <u>menos que</u> mi hermano***. I weigh one kilogram less than my brother.

6. ***Mis abuelos viven <u>más lejos que</u> mis padres***. My grandparents live farther than my parents.

7. ***Gano <u>más de</u> mil dólares en este trabajo.*** I earn more than a thousand dollars in this job.

8. ***Esa bolsa es <u>más grande que</u> esta.*** That bag is bigger than this.

9. ***Eres <u>más alta que</u> tu padre.*** You are taller than your father.

10. ***Esa cama es <u>más pesada que</u> este sofá.*** That bed is heavier than this sofá.

Equality: The two elements of the comparison have the same value.

Tan / Tanto-s + *Adjective/Adverb* + ***como***

Igual de + *Adjective/Adverb* + ***que***

Lo mismo que

With nouns we use ***tanto***

Example:

1. ***La niña es tan hermosa como su mamá***. The girl is as beautiful as her mom.
2. ***El perro es tan peludo como un oso.*** The dog is as hairy as a bear.
3. ***Una casa es igual de cara que un carro***. A house is just as expensive as a car.
4. ***El vuelo cuesta lo mismo que la entrada al concierto***. The flight costs the same as the ticket to the concert.

5. ***Mi suegra tiene <u>tantos</u> zapatos <u>como</u> yo***. My mother-in-law has as many shoes as I do.

6. ***Tú bebes <u>tanta</u> cerveza <u>como</u> mi tío Carlos***. You drink as much beer as my uncle Carlos.

7. ***Este tomate pesa <u>lo mismo que</u> esta naranja***. This tomato weighs the same as this orange.

8. ***Tengo <u>tantos</u> amigos <u>como</u> tú***. I have as many friends as you.

9. ***Este campo de fútbol es <u>igual de</u> grande que un estadio.*** This football field is as big as a stadium.

10. ***El niño es <u>tan cariñoso como</u> su papá.*** The child is as loving as his dad.

Common Errors

Day 45. Most Common Errors

To err is of humans and we can learn from mistakes, but now I want to warn you about some common mistakes that many commit when they learn Spanish and you can avoid.

1. Use the indefinite article un /una /uno /unos /unas before otro /otra /otros /otras.

> I would like another glass of wine.
>
> *Me gustaría* <u>*una otra*</u> *copa de vino. (Incorrect)*
>
> *Me gustaría otra copa de vino. (Correct)*

> Do you have another car?
>
> *¿Tienes* <u>*un otro*</u> *carro? (Incorrect)*
>
> *¿Tienes otro carro? (Correct)*

2. Skip the article el, la, las, los.

I like apples.

Me gustan [...] manzanas. (Incorrect)

Me gustan las manzanas. (Correct)

Family is the most important.

[...] Familia es lo más importante. (Incorrect)

La familia es lo más importante. (Correct)

3. Gender agreement. It is gender equality and number between adjective or article and noun, and the equality of number and person between the verb and the subject.

La casa. The house. *Los niños.* The children. *La novia.* The bride. *Las mesas.* The tables. *El carro.* The car. *Los pájaros.* The birds. *Las montañas.* The mountains. *El gato.* The cat. *La silla.* The chair. *La niña.* The girl. *El hombre.* The man. *Las botellas.* The bottles.

Una casa bonita. A pretty house. *Un perro grande.* A big dog. *Un paisaje bonito.* A beautiful landscape.

There are some exceptions to the rule of gender agreement.

La azúcar (Incorrect)
El azúcar. The sugar.

La agua (Incorrect)
El agua. The water.

El leche (Incorrect)
La leche. The milk.

El moto (Incorrect)
La moto. The bike.

El invitación (Incorrect)
La invitación. The invitation

4. Both words **primero** (first) and **tercero** (third) change when they go before a masculine noun.

Primero juego (Incorrect)
Primer juego. First game.

Tercero nivel (Incorrect)
Tercer nivel. Third level.

Primero premio (Incorrect)
Primer Premio. First Prize

5. Comparative adverb **"más"**. Another common mistake is to use the adverb **más** before adjectives that are comparatives themselves. Such as **peor, mejor, mayor, menor**, or **antes, después, luego**.

I am the oldest.
Soy la más mayor (Incorrect)
Soy la mayor. (Correct)

This wheel is worse than that.

Esta rueda está más peor que aquella (Incorrect)

Esta rueda está peor que aquella. (Correct)

See you later.

Nos vemos más luego (Incorrect)

Nos vemos luego. (Correct)

I am the oldest of my brothers.

Soy la más mayor de mis hermanos (Incorrect)

Soy la mayor de mis hermanos. (Correct)

6. Do not conjugate the verb to the correct form.

I am studying Spanish lessons.

Yo estar estudiando lecciones de español. (Incorrect)

Yo estoy estudiando lecciones de español. (Correct)

I like cold drinks.

***Me gustar* bebidas frías. (Incorrect)**

Me gustan las bebidas frías. (Correct)

She cooks very good.

***Ella cocinar* muy bien. (Incorrect)**

Ella cocina muy bien. (Correct)

You like to travel.

***Te gustar* viajar. (Incorrect)**

Te gusta viajar. (Correct)

Conclusion

Please, read my concluding words in Spanish and try to think in Spanish.

Llegaste a la meta y ahora estás listo para seguir aprendiendo, mejorando tu nivel de español y practicando lo que has aprendido. Espero que no pierdas la oportunidad de hablar español con un hablante nativo.

Con este manual aprendiste español en pocos minutos diariamente, y podrás revisar cualquier lección en sólo pocos minutos también. Puedes llevar este libro contigo y consultar palabras, frases y la gramática en cualquier momento, así te sentirás más seguro. Tu seguridad es importante para que expreses lo que aprendiste.

Felicidades por tu perseverancia, te deseo lo

mejor y que continues mejorando tu español.

Now in English:

You have reached the goal, and now you are ready to continue learning and improving your level of Spanish, and putting what you´ve learned into practice. I hope you do not miss any opportunity to speak with native Spanish speakers.

With this guide, you learned Spanish daily in just a few minutes, and you will be able to review any lesson in just a few minutes too. You can take this book with you anywhere and consult words, phrases, and grammar anytime, so you will feel more secure. Your safety is important for you to express what you have learned.

Congratulations for your perseverance, I wish you the best and continue improving your Spanish.

References

Basic Grammar For The Use Of Spanish.

http://users.jyu.fi/~torremor/cursos/gramatica/001.html

Use of Simple Conditional

<http://www.timandangela.org.uk/spanish/19-condicional-simple>

Woodward English

<https://www.grammar.cl/Present/Simple.htm>

Real Spanish Academy

<http://www.rae.es/>

Literatura y Lingüística. Versión impresa ISSN 0716-5811. Núm 31, Santiago 2015

<https://scielo.conicyt.cl/scielo.php?script=sci_artte
xt&pid=S0716-58112015000100011>

Disclaimer

The information contained in **"Daily Spanish Lessons"** and its components, is meant to serve as a comprehensive collection of strategies that the author of this book has done research about. Summaries, strategies, tips and tricks are only recommendations by the author, and reading this book will not guarantee that one's results will exactly mirror the author's results.

The author of this book has made all reasonable efforts to provide current and accurate information for the readers of this book. The author and its associates will not be held liable for any unintentional errors or omissions that may be found.

The material in the book may include information by third parties. Third party materials comprise of opinions expressed by their owners. As such, the author of this book does not assume responsibility or liability for any third party material or opinions.

The publication of third party material does not constitute the author's guarantee of any information, products, services, or opinions contained within third party material. Use of third party material does not guarantee that your results will mirror our results. Publication of such third party material is simply a recommendation and expression of the author's own opinion of that material.

Whether because of the progression of the Internet, or the unforeseen changes in company policy and editorial submission guidelines, what is stated as fact at the time of this writing may become outdated or inapplicable later.

written expressed and signed permission from the author.